Design With Cricut

The Beginner's Guide To Putting Your Ideas Into Action

Sally R. Ball

Design With Cricut

Bluesource And Friends

This book is brought to you by Bluesource And Friends, a happy book publishing company.

Our motto is **"Happiness Within Pages"**

We promise to deliver amazing value to readers with our books.

We also appreciate honest book reviews from our readers.

Connect with us on our Facebook page www.facebook.com/bluesourceandfriends and stay tuned to our latest book promotions and free giveaways.

Don't forget to claim your FREE books!

Brain Teasers:

https://tinyurl.com/karenbrainteasers

Harry Potter Trivia:

https://tinyurl.com/wizardworldtrivia

Sherlock Puzzle Book (Volume 2)

https://tinyurl.com/Sherlockpuzzlebook2

Also check out our best seller book

"67 Lateral Thinking Puzzles"

https://tinyurl.com/thinkingandriddles

Description

This book was designed to get a Cricut beginner the knowledge to get started making successful projects right after completing this book. This book offers detailed information on everything a Cricut beginner will need to get started. Not only will the reader get a better understanding of what all you can expect from the Cricut hardware and software, including Design Space and Cricut Access, but you will also have the materials and tools used with the Cricut cutting machines described in detail for its uses and functions. A general overview of what this book includes:

- What the Cricut Machine is and how it functions. Ready to start crafting but feel intimidated by the machine itself? This section helps to eliminate all fears that are associated with the machine.
- Tools and Accessories needed to produce your project. This section gives a better understanding of the tools and accessories designed by Cricut to help ensure you have a smooth production of your project from start to finish.
- Materials that can be used in both the Cricut Explore machines and the Cricut maker machines. The Cricut Maker can utilize the same materials as the Cricut Explore, but it

Design With Cricut

    also has more material opens than the Explore. The Maker can even cut the leather to design your own bags and jewelry!

- Project ideas are included for each type of machine to help jump-start the creative process. The first project has easy difficulty while the second can be considered more difficult. As you progress in your projects with Cricut, you will be able to master all levels of difficulty.

- Additional tips and tricks for a Cricut beginner to get started. Learn from the mistakes and realizations of others ahead of the game so you can hit the ground running once you start your first project! These are easily the most tried and true tips and tricks that are guaranteed to help you be a successful Cricut user.

Ultimately we hope this book gives you a better understanding of what the Cricut machine is, what you can do with it, and how to become a successful crafter. This book is a guiding light to all things Cricut and we hope you find it enjoyable and useful for your new found Cricut exploration. Refer back to this book as many times as needed if you are looking for a refresher or are not sure what specific materials you can use with which machine. We provide all this information for you in one convenient place.

Design With Cricut

Table of Contents

Introduction

Chapter 1: What is Cricut?

Chapter 2: Tools and Accessories

    Cricut Explore Cutting Blades

    Cricut Maker Cutting Blades

    Cutting Mats

    The Circuit Weeder

    The Cricut Scraper

    The Cricut Spatula

    The Cricut Tweezers

    The Cricut Scissors

    The Cricut Scoring Tool

    The Cricut Easy press

    The Cricut Brightpad

    The Cricut Cuttlebug Machine

Chapter 3: Materials for the Cricut Machine

    Vinyl

Design With Cricut

Iron-On

Paper

Chipboard

Leather

Fabric

Basswood

Felt

Amazon

Craft Stores: Michaels, JoAnn's, Hobby Lobby

Cricut Website

Chapter 4: Project Ideas

Vinyl

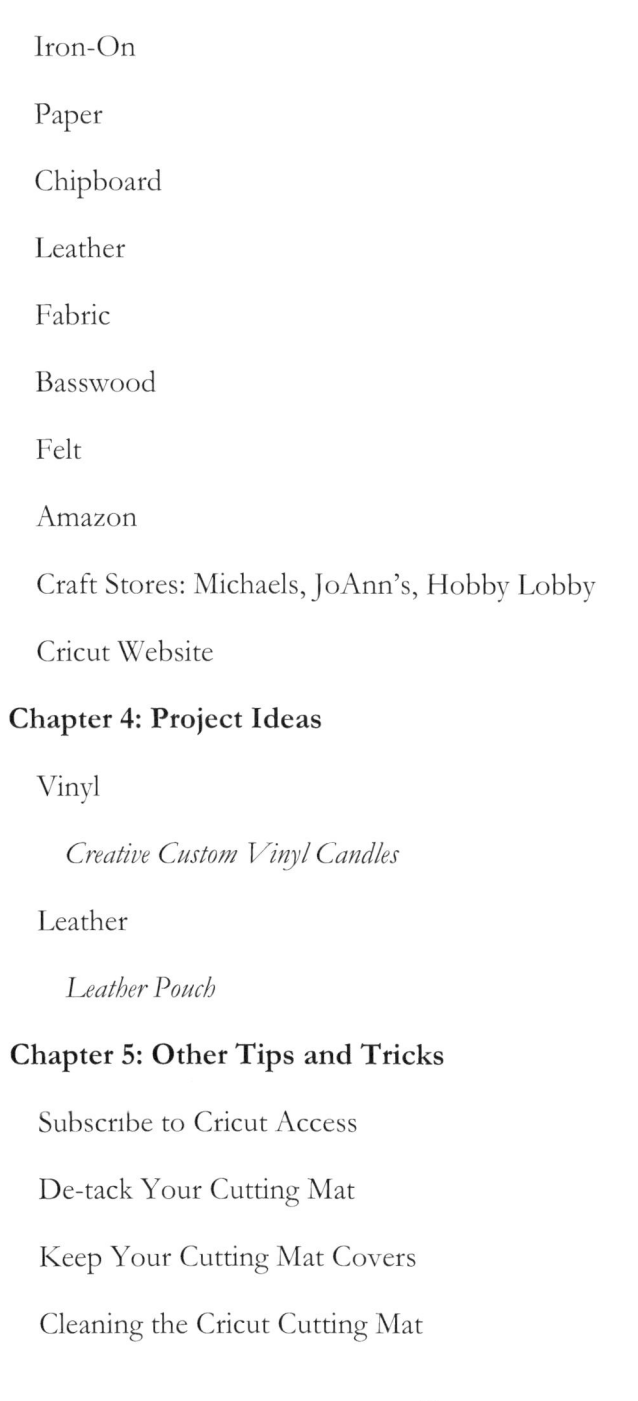

Creative Custom Vinyl Candles

Leather

Leather Pouch

Chapter 5: Other Tips and Tricks

Subscribe to Cricut Access

De-tack Your Cutting Mat

Keep Your Cutting Mat Covers

Cleaning the Cricut Cutting Mat

Design With Cricut

The Right Tools Make all the Difference

Scoring Stylus

Begin with a Sample Project

Test Cuts

Replace Pen Caps after Use

Removing Material from Your Mat

Invest in a Deep Cut Blade

Save Money using Free SVG Files

Other Pens work with the Explore Air Machine

Conclusion

Introduction

Congratulations on getting *Design with Cricut* and thank you for doing so! I recommend reading the machine's user manual prior to reading this book. This will give you a better understanding of the terms and phrases I will be using throughout this book. You can find your manual in the machine's box, or on the Cricut website, where there is loads of useful information for all types of machines.

The following chapters will begin with discussing what the Cricut is; tools and accessories to use with your machine, as well as the materials you can cut using your Cricut. It is important to know what tools and accessories to use with your Cricut to cut down on your preparation time and save yourself a lot of headaches! The Circuit machine is very versatile and can be used with many types of materials to assemble any time of project you can think up. This machine is great for creative minds who love giving personalized and homemade gifts! The book will conclude with project ideas to get you started using your machine, and some final tips and tricks. Learning from the mistakes of others will give you the confidence you need to get started! The Cricut machine can be intimidated at

Design With Cricut

first, but after you conclude this book you will likely be a Pro! You will be on your way to creating beautiful projects in no time!

There are plenty of books on this subject on the market, thanks again for choosing this one! Every effort was made to ensure it's full of as much useful information as possible. Please enjoy!

Chapter 1: What is Cricut?

Cricut is a brand name for a variety of products referred to as home die cutting machines. These machines are used for scrapbooking and other countless creative projects. Cricut is one of the most popular among several electronic die cutters used by scrapbookers, paper crafters, and card makers. Cricut machines are designed to cut paper, vinyl, felt, balsa wood, and various types of fabrics. The Cricut logo is a play on an animated cricket bug, which the name closely represents. The Cricut logo is used throughout their different design offerings, including Cricut Design Space, and Cricut Access.

When the Cricut was introduced, it gave crafters all over the world a long sought after tool for Do It Yourself project in a new, fun, and innovative way. It gave people a new opportunity to approach their projects and creativity. Cricut now influences passion and originality in a way that people truly enjoy! People all over the world have been able to make successful businesses from their Cricut design which brings more and more people to the world of Cricut crafting each and every year. Now is the perfect time to get started using the Circuit machine if this is something you want to obtain for yourself, and this book will help you get there.

Design With Cricut

Cricut Models

There are three current models of Cricut cutters, the Explore Air, Explore Air 2, and the Cricut Maker. All three of these models are compatible with the current Circuit Design Space plugin for your computer.

The Explore Air is the oldest model, but it offers a wireless or Bluetooth connection to your computer that hosts your Design Space. This machine can cut a variety of materials including paper, vinyl, fabric and more.

Next in line is the Explore Air 2 machine, which is a minor upgrade from the original Explore Air offering. It added three colors to the collection; Mint Blue, Rose Anna, and Giffin Lilac. This model also offers a Fast Mode that allows users to cut vinyl, iron-on, and cardstock up to two times faster than the original Explore Air machine.

The final and newest offering from Cricut is the Maker model. This model was released in August of 2017. It was designed to cut thicker materials such as Balsawood, Basswood, leather, felt, and non-bonded fabrics. The Maker model is the only Cricut machine designed to use a Rotary Blade, to cutting fabric directly, as well as a scoring wheel that has variable pressure levels to score thicker cardstock papers than the original scoring stylus previously used.

All three of these machines also allow crafters an option for adding an element of writing and drawing to their creations. This is made possible loading a pen or marker into the accessory slot. When doing this, the machine will follow any design you desire. The Cricut is a proven multifaceted machine that is designed to bring a new level of versatility to any project.

How does it Work?

If you are using a Cricut machine for the first time with little to no experience, it can be a bit overwhelming. When looking at the machine as a type of printer, this can help users get a better understanding of how the machine actually works. When you see a completed design created by a Cricut machine, it is hard to imagine it was not created by a professional. In fact, many long-time users of the Cricut machines have started and continue to run extremely successful creative businesses online. You too could also be on your way to earning a lucrative side income once you get the groundwork for learning how the Cricut operates.

Design Space

To access the Cricut Design Space online catalog of clip art, fonts, and premade designs all you need is access to a computer or tablet and the internet. Something that Cricut recently started doing with the Design Space platform was to create a plug-in option for PC and Mac users. This way, you can access Design Space without ever having to open an internet web browser. This cuts down on wait time and issues with connectivity. Design Space is now also offered as an app to users, whether you are an iPhone or Android user, there is an option for all. Crafters can now design on the go, wherever they are in the world. See a design you like while window shopping? You can instantly upload a similar design to your Design Space workplace, and save it until you are able to give it the attention it deserves, all on your phone in an instant! You can also customize any premade design uploaded to Design Space, to suit your needs and make it your own.

Start with an Idea

Design With Cricut

Want to get crafting but have no idea where to start? Design space offers a wide variety of project ideas to get your creative mind turning. Design Space is set up to show your current working projects at the very top of the page, and different project ideas by category as you scroll down the page. Each project varies in level of difficulty. If you see a project you would like to try, simply click on it and it will provide more detail on how to get started. The details should include the level of difficulty, materials needed to complete the project, and how long it should take you to finish the project. It will also tell you who uploaded the design idea. If you like the designs done by a particular user, you will be able to see all projects that have been uploaded by this user.

Some project ideas include:

- Ready-to-make
    - These projects are already designed and crafted. All you have to do is gather your supplies and you are well on your way to a brand new custom made Tote bag (for example)!

- Cards
    - Design Space offers a variety of holiday cards as well as birthday, get well soon, and congratulatory events

Design With Cricut

- Home Décor
  - Wreaths, Pillow Cases, Mobiles, and Wall Art will be located here

- Monograms
  - You will have a lot of design options when it comes to making a monogram. These can include, Iron-on clothing, Window Clings, and Coasters just to name a few

- Quilts
  - If you have the Cricut Maker machine, there is a wide variety of quilt designs to get you started. The Maker machine provides everything you need to create a homemade quilt to give as a gift or to keep around your home when the weather gets cold.

- Sewing
  - This can include embroidery and creating your own clothing. There are many premade designs for shirts, skirts, and purses readily available for all Design Space users

Design With Cricut

Machine Set Up and Use

Initially, you will want to set up and do practices run on the machine before starting any of your own projects. Cricut will provide detailed instructions as well as practice material to help get you started. It is important that you take the time to do this step so that your machine is properly calibrated, and you are able to view the multiple functions before getting started.

Once you have your design picked out and your materials gathered you would want to make sure that your machine is set correctly to ensure your project will be cut perfectly. Depending on the type of material you are using, you will want to adjust the dial on the machine to the correct function. For instance, if you are using cardstock, you will want the function set to cardstock, not iron-on. This is because different cutting materials with have different levels of thickness, and you do not want to have the machine set to a function that will not properly cut all the way through your material the first time, and vice versa, a thick setting will rip through your thin materials and could potentially ruin the entire project resulting in you having to start over completely.

Design With Cricut

The newest Cricut machines now have two connectivity options. You can pair your device to your Cricut machine via Bluetooth, or you also have the option to hard wire the machine to your device, in the event Bluetooth connectivity is not an option. Either way, both options give you a seamless connection from your device to your Cricut machine. If your Bluetooth connection is available, it will automatically engage once you are on the cut design screen. You will be able to know that your connection is available as the Cut button on your Cricut Machine will turn blue. If the button is not blue, the Bluetooth connection is not engaged. Once you are on the cut screen, Bluetooth is connected and the correct material function is selected, you are officially ready to be cutting your project.

You will repeat this process with each project you create. If you are adding a writing element to your design, the only additional step you will have to ensure is done would be to put your chosen writing utensil in the accessory slot. Do not worry if for some reason you forget to do this. As long as you have the writing option selected in your design, Design Space will remind you to add the writing utensil to the accessories slot when it is time to start that part of the design. Design Space makes crafting a breeze; there should virtually be no issues when designing with Cricut!

Design With Cricut

Chapter 2: Tools and Accessories

In this section, we will discuss the must-have tools for each of the Cricut Explore machines as well as the additional tools that will be needed for the Cricut Maker Machine. There are very few supplies you need to get started using your Cricut Explore, and they will come in the package when you buy even the most basic Cricut Explore package—so you do not have to buy anything extra at the beginning! These two included Cricut accessories are a cutting mat and a carbide blade. Everything else is optional, but allows you to do even more with this amazing machine! Typically if you purchase your machine directly from Cricut, they will have a "bundle" option that includes additional tools and accessories, and sometimes even their branded cutting materials to help get you started. Let's check them out!

Cricut Explore Cutting Blades

Both Cricut Explore Machines come with an extremely sharp German carbide fine-point blade. This allows all users to get started cutting right away. It comes already housed within the Cricut machine and is easily removable and sharpened in the event that the blade gets dull. A user tip on keeping your blade sharp and long-lasting is to stick the blade into a ball of aluminum foil to sharpen it. This allows you to continue using the same blade for an extended period of time, and saving you money as well! A fine- point cutting blade is typically used for almost all of the Cricut design cutting projects, and will last through many projects when taken care of properly. If you are continually cutting rough materials, it is recommended to sharpen the blade often, or you will find yourself replacing it more often. The housing for this blade is silver on the older style machines and has been upgraded to gold for the new generation of machines.

The next type of blade that is commonly used is the Deep Cut blade. This is the type of blade you will need in order to cut thicker materials. These materials include thin wood and leather. You heard that right; you can cut leather with a Cricut machine! With this blade, you will need to get its custom housing piece, which you can purchase separately. When using this blade, you will simply need to swap out the housing pieces and then attach the blade as necessary. Similarly, as the fine-point blade, you will need to take care of this blade and sharpen it often. Since you are using thick materials for this blade, you may have to replace it more often if using it all the time. The housing for this type of cut blade is black. You also will have the option to purchase cut blades individually once you have the housing unit.

Finally, there is a Bonded Fabric cut blade. You will use this blade to cut a variety of fabrics once it has been stabilized with Heat N Bond or some other type of stabilizer. This precision cutting tool stays sharper longer and can also be used with a fabric that has iron-on. It is made from premium German carbide steel. It is specifically designed to make intricate cuts with the Cricut machines. This blade is identifiable with its pink color.

Cricut Maker Cutting Blades

In addition to the Explore Cutting blade, the Cricut Maker has additional cutting blades that allow for intricate cutting details on a variety of materials.

The Knife blade was released in August of 2017. The Knife Blade was designed to cut thicker and denser materials that cannot be easily or successfully cut with other blades. These materials include Balsa Wood, Basswood, Cricut Chipboard, Craft foam, leather, and Matboard. When cutting with the Knife blade, Cricut Design space will ask you if you wish to add one more cut pass, to get a complete cut. This is typically recommended when using thick wood and metal materials.

The Cricut Maker comes with one additional blade, the revolutionary rotary cutting blade for use on cutting all sorts of fabrics. Unlike the average rotary blade, this one lasts far longer because it avoids the nicks that typically come with its line of duty. You can buy additional blades individually, but one blade should last throughout multiple projects.

Cutting Mats

Cricut cutting mats come in a variety of sizes and degree of stickiness. Depending on what material you are using, you will want less or more stickiness on your mat, to hold the material in place while cutting.

Standard grip Mats can be used for most of your project cutting needs. You are able to cut cardstock, vinyl, and iron-on, etc. with this mat. This mat is included in the box with any Cricut cutting machine purchase in the green 12"x12" style.

If you are using more delicate materials like vellum or light paper, you will want to invest in a Light grip cutting mat. Similarly, if you are using cutting heavier materials that have a tendency to shift, you will want to invest in a Strong grip cutting mat. Standard grip, Light grip, and Strong grip cutting mats also come in a 12"x24" size mat.

There is also a Pink Fabric cutting mat, something that is necessary when cutting any time of fabric with a Cricut Maker machine. It comes in a 12"x12" size or a 12"x24" size, depending on how large your project cut is. The adhesive on the Cricut pink mat is more delicate than on the other mats. The oils in your fingers quickly break down the adhesive in the mat, causing it to lose its stick. Just be cautious with your mat and try to avoid touching the adhesive if possible. Use tweezers when trying to pick pieces up off of your mat.

No matter what cutting mat you use, it is suggested to break it in a little bit before you use it for the first time. Take off the clear mat protector and stick the mat to the front of your shirt a few times. It will pick up some of the lint and, believe it or not, this will help drastically when removing your project from the mat after it's been cut. It's nearly impossible to remove a project cleanly from a brand-spanking new mat, regardless of what type of material you are using.

The Circuit Weeder

The weeder tool, which looks similar to a dental pick, is used for removing negative space from a vinyl project. This weeder tool is a *must* when doing any type of project that involves vinyl. Trying to get rid of access vinyl is nearly impossible without a weeder especially with materials like glitter iron-on. A weeder is a useful tool for any type of project using adhesives. Instead of picking up the adhesive with your fingertips, user the weeder tool and keep your fingers sticky mess free!

The Cricut Scraper

The Circuit Scraper tool is essential (and a lifesaver!) when you need to rid your cutting mat of excess negative bits. This tool typically works best with paper, such as cardstock, but other materials can easily be scraped up as well. Use the flexibility of the mat to your advantage as you scrap the bits off the mat, to ensure you are not scraping up the adhesive on the mat as well. You can also use the Cricut Scraper as a score line holder, which allows you to fold over the scoreline with a nice crisp edge. It can also be used as a burnishing tool for Cricut transfer tape, as it will allow seamless separation of the transfer tape from the backing.

The Cricut Spatula

A spatula is a must-have tool for a crafter who works with a lot of paper. Pulling the paper off of a Cricut cut mat can result in a lot of tearing and paper curling if you are not diligent and mindful when you are removing it. The spatula is thinly designed to slip right under paper which allows you to ease it off the mat carefully. Be sure to clean it often as it is likely to get the adhesive build up on it after multiple uses. It can also be used as a scraper if your scraper tool is not readily available!

The Cricut Tweezers

Projects that involve a lot of embellishments will require a pair of tweezers. The Cricut tweezers can be a bit awkward to use at first, as they function directly opposite than we are used to with traditional tweezers. They need to be squeezed to open them, as opposed to squeezing them to shut. Ultimately you will begin to realize the genius behind this design because you will be able to pick something up and release pressure on it as the Cricut tweezers will hold pressure on the object. You'll save yourself from continuously dropping small pieces, and many hand cramps!

The Cricut Scissors

Using the right scissors for a job can make a world of difference. The Cricut Scissors are made from stainless steel to ensure they will stick around for many jobs before getting dull. The scissors come with a micro-tip blade, so finer details in smaller areas are easier and clean right down to a point.

The Cricut Scoring Tool

If you want to do projects that involve a scoring line, such as folding cards in half or making 3D boxes, you will want to invest in a Cricut Scoring tool. You can insert this tool into the second tool holder, or accessory clamp, into the Cricut Explore itself, and the Cricut will use it to make score lines wherever the design dictates. They will need to be present in the Cricut Design Space file in order for the machine to recognize the scoreline is needed in the project. The basic tool kit sold by Cricut does not come with a scoring tool you will need to purchase this separately. If you plan to work with a lot of paper projects, this is a worthy tool to invest in.

The Cricut Easy press

If you begin to venture into iron-on projects and want to upgrade from a traditional iron and ironing board, the Cricut Easypress is the right way to go. It will make projects so much easier than using a traditional iron. The Cricut Easypress is known to help keep designed adhered for longer, essentially no more peeling of designs after one or two uses and washes. The Easypress also takes all of the guesswork out of the right amount of contact time as well as temperature. You will not run the risk of burning your transfer paper or fabric!

The Cricut Brightpad

The lightweight and low profile design of the Cricut Brightpad reduces eyestrain while making crafting easier. It is designed to illuminate fine lines for tracing, cut lines for weeding and so much more! It is thin and lightweight which allows for durable transportation. BrightPad makes crafting more enjoyable with its adjustable, evenly lit surface. The bright LED lights can be adjusted depending on the workspace. The only downfall to this accessory is that it must be plugged in while it is used. It does not contain a rechargeable battery.

The Cricut Cuttlebug Machine

The Cricut Cuttlebug is embossing and dies cutting machine that offers portability and versatility when it comes to cutting and embossing a wide variety of materials. This machine gives

Design With Cricut

professional looking results with clean, crisp, and deep embosses. This machine goes beyond paper, allowing you to emboss tissue paper, foils, thin leather, and more!

We sincerely hope this section gives you a better understanding of the tools and accessories that can be used with the Cricut cutting machines and how best to put them into use when designing and creating your own projects! Know that these tools are here to make your life easier it's worth investing in them!

Chapter 3: Materials for the Cricut Machine

Most people believe that they can only cut paper and vinyl with the Cricut machine. You will soon find once you get started using your machine that it can actually cut over 100 different types of materials! In this section, we will go over a variety of them in detail to get a better understanding of how truly remarkable the Cricut machine really is! Get inspired by a collection of diverse, high-quality materials, all designed to cut perfectly with Cricut machines. Material finishes ranging from fun and flashy, to polished and rich. These materials make it easy to achieve exactly the look you are after. Once you get more comfortable using all the different types of materials, you will easily be able to create projects that have multiple materials in one! Utilize resources such as this book to refer to when you have questions relating to what type of material to use and when. The more you know, the better your project will be!

Vinyl

Adhesive vinyl for Cricut cutting machines come in a wide variety of colors, designs, and uses. The adhesive properties can either be semi-permanent (easily removable with adhesive remover) or permanent.

Semi-permanent is typically used for projects indoors, such as wall decals or window clings. Permanent vinyl would be used for outdoor use, such as holiday décor and tabletop designs. Vinyl is the most commonly used material for Cricut projects outside of paper because it is one of the most versatile materials to work with. Adhesive vinyl is a great starting point for creators who are new to Cricut but want to branch out outside of paper crafting. Adhesive vinyl is a material that will need to be weeded, as designs are typically cut out of the vinyl and the negative space will need to be removed in order to see the design. This book will offer vinyl project ideas in the next chapter.

Iron-On

Iron-On vinyl is a special type of vinyl that is adhered to a surface using a heat sensitive adhesive. It can be used on fabric and other materials such as wood paper and metal. There are many how-to videos online for Iron-On Vinyl because it can be a tricky material to work with. More often than not, when using Iron-On Vinyl you will need to use the "Mirror" feature in Design Space. This feature allows you to cut your vinyl backward so that when you go to apply heat to the design, it will show the correct way on your surface. Luckily for us, Cricut builds in a feature for Design Space that reminds you to turn on the mirror option when the dial is set to iron on. You can easily and quickly waste a lot of material if your image is not set to mirror! Iron on vinyl is most commonly permanent as this type of material is usually used with fabrics. There are numbers videos on how to remove iron on shortly after application if you do make a mistake, however! Utilizing how-to videos is an important part of getting comfortable with using this type of Cricut material. This book will offer different iron-on project ideas in the next chapter.

Paper

There is a wide variety of paper products that can be cut using the Cricut machine. Some varieties include cardstock, which is one of the most popular, corrugated cardboard, foil embossed, Kraft board, scrapbooking paper, pearl, sparkle/shimmer, and poster board. Paper products can come in a wide range of sizes, with 12"x12" being the most common and easily applied type as it fits perfectly on a 12"x12" cutting mat. Paper is most commonly used in card projects, but it can also assist in wall décor, gift boxes, cake toppers, lantern projects. Most crafters familiar with the Cricut recommend starting with the paper project first, to get a handle of the different options Cricut cutters to have. Paper allows you to create intricate designs and get familiar with cutting blade depth at the same time. This book will offer different paper project ideas in the next chapter.

The following materials can only be used with the Cricut Maker machine.

Chipboard

Chipboard, also known as a type of particle board, is an engineered wood product that has been manufactured from saw shavings, wood chips, and a synthetic resin, which is pressed and extruded. The Cricut website sells a variety pack of this type of material, which is great for getting to know the material and what projects to use it effectively. It is suggested for use on projects such as sturdy wall art, school projects, photo frames and more. Since this material has a 1.5mm thickness, it can only be cut using the Cricut Knife blade. Chipboard is great for any time of project that requires dimensions such as gingerbread or haunted house around the holidays! This book will offer different chipboard project ideas in the next chapter.

Leather

Have you ever dreamt of becoming a famous purse or leather goods designer? You can now make that dream a reality with the Cricut Maker! Cricut offers a few different color options for genuine leather. You will love the look and feel of real leather for your projects! It has a supple feel, smooth surface, and rich color, perfect for fashion, accessories, jewelry, and more. There is always the option to mix and match colors and styles for impressively dimensional projects! Leather is one of the newest options for Cricut Maker materials, but it is quickly becoming a favorite among users! Leather will always be in style, so if you are someone who loves to create their own unique fashion looks, this material will be the right one for you and all your design needs! This book will offer different leather project ideas in the next chapter.

Fabric

This simple yet classic material is another favorite among Cricut Maker users. Many use fabric to create custom clothing, home décor, and wall art. Imagine all the times you went out looking for the perfect top or skirt only to come back home empty handed after many hours of searching. It would be ideal to find exactly what you want when you want it! Now, without the help of a bulky and outdated sewing machine, you can make simple and affordable clothing exactly the look and feel you want! Fabric is also a great material to make homemade gifts for friends and family. Lots of people enjoy curling up on the couch during the winter months with a cozy quilt and a favorite movie. Now you can provide the quilt and have long-lasting memories made with it! Friends and family from all over will want in on the action! Quilts will never go out of style, and neither will give them as gifts! This book will offer different fabric project ideas in the next chapter.

Basswood

The final material we will cover in this chapter is Basswood. Similar to balsa wood, but has a much greater thickness. Basswood is a high-quality wood with a tight grain that allows for a smooth and precise finish. Basswood is typically the first choice of wood for wood carvers because of its reliable sturdiness. It is denser than balsa wood. Therefore, it is an ideal surface for clean cuts. This material can be painted and stained easily without having to be stained first. This is a great option for someone who is looking to get into woodworking, but not quite equipped with old-time tricks and tips. You will need to use this material with the Strong grip mat, and tape down all four corners to ensure that it does not shift during cutting. It is perfect for projects including models, toys, dollhouses, home decor, shadow boxes, mixed media art, and more. This book will offer different basswood project ideas in the next chapter.

Felt

Blended fibers between natural and synthetic are also common among craft felts. Felt is commonly used to help young children

Design With Cricut

distinguish among different types of textiles. Felt is also commonly used in craft projects for all ages. The felt is easily cut with your Cricut Machine, no Deep Cut blade required! Felt can be used for fun décor, kid's crafts, baby toys, stuffed shapes and more! When starting out on the Cricut Maker, this is one of the best materials to start out with. This material is very forgiving and will allow you to keep the gift-giving spirit going! This material is also great for creating faux flowers. You can bring the outside in, without the maintenance or worrying about children or pets getting into a mess! This book will offer different felt project ideas in the next chapter.

Now that you have an idea of the variety of materials you can use with both the Cricut Explore machine and the Cricut Maker machine, you are well on your way to creating one of a kind, beautiful works of art! Although this is just a small list of the different materials that are available for use, it is a great starting point for someone who is new to the Cricut world! Once you have mastered these different types of materials you will be able to venture out into new kinds of materials and see the potential both Cricut Explore and Cricut Maker have to offer. It is good also to know which types of materials you feel that you would like to work with the most to determine which machine is right for you.

It is also good for beginners to know where the best places to buy these materials are. Although Cricut sells the majority of the materials you need to get started, there are many other places you are able to buy materials from. Below we will list the different places you should be able to buy any Cricut material you will need.

Amazon

Amazon has become a leader in providing materials for Cricut projects, at a much lower cost than the Cricut website. Amazon also offers a wide variety of brands all that is compatible with both the Cricut Explore machine and the Cricut Maker machine. Amazon also offers free two-day shipping for Prime Members; many of these items are included in the offer. This is a great option for new crafters that may need materials in a hurry, depending on the type of project they are doing and when they would like to begin. Amazon is a great resource for finding new material offerings and brands that carry them. It doesn't hurt to save money on a project and receive free shipping as well!

Craft Stores: Michaels, JoAnn's, and Hobby Lobby

If you are someone who enjoys going to a store to purchase items for a project over ordering them online, you too have many options to purchase your materials from. Craft stores have been around for a long time, but they have just recently started providing materials for all the Cricut Machines. You can easily think of a project and run to your nearest craft store and get everything you need to get started on your project that day. This also comes in handy if you are missing something you thought you had, or run out of something you need right away. These stores are always in convenient locations and making material gathering easy for everyone!

Cricut Website

As mentioned before, Cricut online also provides a great resource for buying materials for your Cricut projects. They keep their products up to date and often offer products that are created by designers. This is a great option for materials that are unlike what is sold in-store and online. Another great perk of buying directly from Cricut is that if you are a Design Space member, you will receive 10% off every purchase you make through them. Cricut takes care of their customers in more ways than one!

Chapter 4: Project Ideas

In this section of the book, we will go over a few project ideas in for each material listed in the previous chapter to get you started working with your Cricut machine. As you become more familiar with your Cricut machine you will become more creative, and you will soon find yourself coming up with new project ideas all day long. The Cricut website and Design Space are both great tools for project ideas to help get you started if you are not sure what type of project you would like to begin. Pinterest is also another great online resource for project ideas at different levels of difficulty.

Always keep in mind when starting a new project that you first must have all of the materials necessary to complete the project. It is always helpful to review your stock of tools and materials before getting started. The worst feeling is when you sit down and begin working on a difficult project only to realize you are out of a specific material needed to finish the job. It will save you a lot of time in the long run if you spend a few minutes at the beginning taking stock of your inventory! Working with materials you already have on hand is also a great way to keep your crafting costs low. It will always feel good to know that you made a custom piece of work without spending a ton of extra money just to complete it!

Vinyl

This section will begin with a vinyl project idea to help get you started working with this type of material.

Creative Custom Vinyl Candles

Supplies Needed:

- Cricut Essential Tool Set
- Cutting Mat
- Transfer Tape

Step One: Pick your Quote and Design it in Design Space

Depending on the size of the candle you are using, you will want to keep your quote small and simple. Be sure to select a font that is easy to read. There are many different quote options already predesigned in Design space that you will have immediate access to. You will also have access to quite a few more design ideas for free if you are a Cricut Access Member. Once you have decided on a design, you should import it to your design mat. Here you can change the font size, color, and script. Once you have your design just as you want it, you can move on to the next step!

Design With Cricut

Step Two: Measure, Cut and Place Vinyl on your Mat

You will want to start this project by selecting the type of vinyl you want to use, in this project I would recommend permanent vinyl. You will then want to grab your 12"x12" mat with either standard or light grip. This type of mat usually works best with vinyl material. You will want to line up the vinyl to the grid on the cutting mat. This grid lines up with the grid in design space (if you choose to have the grid showing while you design). This will help you minimize waste as you can cut off only the exact amount of material you need to complete this project.

Step Three: Cut Out Vinyl

Before cutting, ensure that your Cricut machine is set to the right setting to cut vinyl. Depending on the type of vinyl you are using, you can select a thin vinyl setting or set the cut to a thicker level, just to ensure that the Cricut machine cuts all the way through the vinyl on the first go round. You will want to back to stay intact, however (this will make weeding a lot easier when you get to this in the next stop) so don't overdo the cut pressure. Once you are secure in your vinyl placement on the mat, as well as your machine setting you are ready to go! Design Space will prompt you to load the mat before cutting.

Design With Cricut

Once the mat is loaded and the cut button on your Cricut Machine is blinking, you are ready to hit the button and begin cutting. Design Space will give you a percentage as to how far into the project it has cut. The more intricate the cut, the longer it will take.

Step Four: Remove Vinyl from Mat and Begin Weeding

This step is where you will need your trusty Cricut Weeder! You will want to remove all of the excess vinyl away from the cut that you want to put on your candle. Weeding can be tedious, and you will either end up loving it or hate it! This part of the project will also take some time depending on how difficult a design you choose. This is also a great step in a project to use your Cricut Bright pad if you have one. This will help illuminate the cut lines and help you differentiate between the excess vinyl and the pieces you want to keep. A wise investment if you truly enjoy intricate cut pieces with lots of weeding!

Step Five: Apply Transfer Tape

Transfer Tape is the material that will allow you to remove your vinyl design from its original backing and place it onto your project surface. The transfer tape will attach to the front of the vinyl, which is not sticky, and pull it from its original backing to expose the sticky side of the vinyl. You will want to ensure your design is fully stuck to the transfer tape before trying to remove it from the original backing. It is strongly recommended to smooth the transfer tape over your original design using your Cricut Scraper. This will also help you remove any air bubbles that may develop during the transfer tape applied to your design. Once you feel your design is securely stuck to the transfer tape, begin removing the design from the original backing.

Step Six: Apply Vinyl to Project Surface

Once your design is removed from the original backing you are ready to apply the design to your project surface via the transfer tape. You will want to follow the same process of smoothing the design onto the surface with your Cricut scraper and removing all of the air bubbles that will likely develop because the surface of a candle is typically curved. This may take some time to do correctly, and transfer tape is usually fairly forgiving if you need to remove the design and reposition it before starting over. Once you feel your design is full stuck onto the project surface, you can begin to slowly remove the transfer tape. It should easily come off of the design, while the design continues to stick to the project surface. If you find that the transfer tape is pulling the design off of the project surface, stop and smooth the design back onto the project surface again with your scraper. You may have to do this a few times before the vinyl will stick. Once you have the vinyl fully stuck with the transfer tape removed, your project is complete!

You will follow a similar guideline for any type of vinyl project you may choose. There will always be adjustments depending on the type of vinyl you are using and the difficulty of the cut. Ultimately if you follow this step by step guide you will easily be creating multiple vinyl projects. Similar vinyl projects include coasters, drink cups, and car window monograms. Vinyl is one of the most versatile materials you can cut with your Cricut Machine. If you can think it, you can design it and cut it! This sample project is a great way to get started in the vinyl world.

Leather

This section will begin with a leather project idea to help get you started working with this type of material.

Leather Pouch

Supplies Needed:

- Cricut Brand Genuine Leather
- X-actor knife or rotary cutter

Design With Cricut

- Deep Cut Blade
- Cricut Strong grip cutting mat
- Scoring Tool
- Heavy Duty Snaps
- Fabric Adhesive

Step One: Set Up Your Machine and Leather on the strong grip cutting mat

The first thing you will need to do is load up your machine with the genuine leather already pressed into a strong grip mat. You will want to place the leather smooth side (face) down on the strong grip mat. You will also want to make sure that the edge of the leather is inside the lines of the strong grip mat. This will ensure that the leather will not bump into the black bumper as it feeds into the machine. You will also want to cut down the right edge of the piece of genuine leather as it only needs to be 11 inches wide. Then you will want to move the four-star wheels or the little white wheels on your Cricut machine, over to the right so that you can run the material without bumping the wheels. Next and most importantly you will want to load your deep cut blade before starting this project. This is the only way to ensure the cut will make it all the way through the genuine leather! You are finally ready to load your mat up!

Design With Cricut

Step Two: Loading the design pattern into Design Space

There is a premade design ready to go with Cricut Access in Design Space. The best thing about Cricut Access premade designs is that all you have to do is hit "make it" and it will load all of the materials settings, there is no need to size it! Select your machine and material. Note: If you are using the Cricut Explore make sure you have the dial turned to Custom in order to get all these options. This is where you will want to load your scoring tool to the accessories slot as well.

Step Three: Hit "Go" and watch the Cricut machine to make magic!

This may take some time, and it is also recommended to go a test piece before running an entire sheet of leather into the machine. It would be a shame to waste a full sheet of material because the machine is not properly set up or there is an issue with the blade. Similar to measure first cut once, always run a test design with scraps left over from previous projects!

Step Four: Add Snaps and Glue in Flaps

You will want to follow the directions on your snap kit to learn how to properly install the snaps on your leather pouch. You can pick one

Design With Cricut

of these kits up at your local fabric store. You will want to glue the flaps in last so that you can ensure it lines up with the snaps secured.

The leather project above gives you a great opportunity to take advantage of the predesigned projects that are readily available with Cricut Access in Design Space. This one does require more technical advantages and has a higher degree of difficulty over the vinyl project also recommended. Safety always comes first, and it is recommended you read through the entire instructions to a project such as this before beginning the project yourself. It is also a good idea to have a helper on hand in the event you will need another pair of hands. Once you have a few practices rounds under your belt you should feel more comfortable doing this project on your own.

We sincerely hope you enjoy these sample projects we have provided for you. These are just two samples of what your new Cricut machine is capable of making. Anything you can dream up is an option for you to make on your Cricut machine, and this probably why the machine has gotten so popular in recent years! Feel free to begin your Cricut journey with these projects and others that are free for Cricut users all over the internet. Always remember that Cricut access is also a great resource for finding premade and designed projects ready to

Design With Cricut

go! We hope this section gives you a better understanding of what Cricut has to offer in terms of project availability.

Chapter 5: Other Tips and Tricks

In this section, we will cover roughly 13 tried and true tips and tricks for Cricut newbies and beginners. This section will help you learn from the mistakes of other Cricut crafters so that you do not have to go through the same trials and tribulations yourself. This section will be like having your very own Cricut expert sitting alongside you! We want you to be able to hit the ground running after you finish this book, so this section is going to do just that! We hope you find the following tips and tricks useful for the many projects you surely will create!

Subscribe to Cricut Access

If you really want to get a full range of use out of both your Cricut Explore machine as well as the Cricut Maker machine we would recommend you subscribe to Cricut Access right away. There are two options for payment. You can either pay a monthly fee of $10, or you can pay one time for the entire year. This works out to be slightly cheaper on a month to month basis. This will give you access to thousands of different predesigned projects as well as Cricut Access exclusive fonts, that you would otherwise have to pay to use. If you are planning to use your Cricut a lot, this will save you a lot of money as opposed to buying every project an image individually. We can all agree it is a lot easier to pay one flat rate instead of having to figure out how much you are actually spending on projects. Get your money's worth out of your Cricut and subscribe to Cricut Access.

De-tack Your Cutting Mat

The Circuit Explore machine will come with a green 12"x12" Standard grip cutting mat. The Cricut Maker machine will come with a blue light grip mat. As you already know, you will place your cutting material onto this mat before inserting it into the machine to cut. As you will come to find out, the green cutting mat is extremely sticky when it is brand new. After you initially peel the plastic covering off for the first time, you will want to place a clean, dry t-shirt on top of the mat to prime it for your first project. It is really hard to get cardstock paper off, even with all of your tools at your disposal, when it has its full stickiness! It is very easy to damage the project, especially paper when you are trying to pull it off the mat.

Keep Your Cutting Mat Covers

The cutting mats that you purchase for your projects will always come brand new with a plastic protecting sheet over it. This can be pulled off and put back on for the entire life of the mat. You will want to keep this plastic cover as long as you have the mat. It will keep the stickiness level up on your mat, and it will make the mat easier to store away when not in use.

Cleaning the Cricut Cutting Mat

It is very important to keep your cutting mat clean in order for it to remain sticky and be available for use over and over. Ideally, you would want to clean the mat every time after use if not at least every couple uses would suffice. All you will have to do is simply wipe down a clean mat with baby wipes to keep it clean. The non-alcohol water-based wipes that are fragrance-free are the best ones to use on your cutting mat. This will keep your mat free of vinyl residue that ultimately builds up as well as cardstock that may have been missed in the initial cleaning process. It will also help keep common household dust and dirt from affecting your mat and projects as well.

The Right Tools Make all the Difference

Often if you buy a Cricut machine bundle it will include the Cricut toolset. If not, you will want to ensure you get at least the basic toolset once you get started using your machine. The toolset contains the weeder, scraper, tweezers, spatula, and scissors that were discussed in detail in the earlier chapter relating to tools and accessories. If you are not ready to make a commitment to all of the tools, it is highly suggested to at least get the weeding tool if you are planning to do any projects with cardstock or vinyl.

Scoring Stylus

Most if not all card projects will require a score line, which is easily created by the scoring stylus. You will want to purchase one of these if you plan on creating a lot of cards with your machine. The scoring stylus creates the fold line that turns a simple cut paper into a beautiful card. If you buy your machine as part of a bundle more often than not this will be included in the bundle, so there is no need to purchase this separately. There are many more uses for the scoring stylus, but making cards are one of its main functions.

Begin with a Sample Project

Once your machine arrives and you've taken the time to open the box and sort through everything that is included, you will notice that Cricut has provided you with a sample project. The Explore Air machine will come with a sample card for you to begin with, for example. You will receive the minimum amount of materials you will need in order to complete the project successfully. It is good practice to start off with something simple, rather than a big and fancy project that can easily become intimidating. Starting here is a great point to get familiar with the hardware and software.

Test Cuts

When starting your own projects it is wise, to begin with, test cuts before trying to cut your entire project. This will help you ensure that you are using the correct settings within Design Space as well as on the machine. Also if your blade is cut too low, you run the risk of cutting into your mat. If the blade is set too high, you likely won't cut through the material all the way. Doing a test cut before each project will help you from making these mistakes and ruining your supplies and wasting material. Check the settings, and make any changes if something isn't right.

Replace Pen Caps after Use

One of the most easily forgotten things that can also save you a lot of money on supplies is remembering to replace your pen caps when you are done using them. It is easy to leave the pen in the accessories clip when you are finishing up a project. This will, in turn, make the pen dry out much faster as a lot of the pens are very inky. If you immediately remove the pen from the clip after the machine is complete and putting on the cap, you will not only extend the life of the pen; you will save yourself money in the long run for not having to replace your pens continually.

Removing Material from Your Mat

Other than using your Cricut tools like your scraper and spatula to get your materials off of your mat, there is another trick that requires no tools at all. Instead of peeling your project from the mat, which usually results in tears and curling of the material, you will want to peel the mat away from your project. What we mean is, bend the mat away from your project instead of the other way around. This can be done by flipping the mat upside down and peeling one of the corners back to start. If needed, you can then slip your spatula under the project to gently lift it up and away from the mat.

Invest in a Deep Cut Blade

There is nothing worse than setting your sights on a highly creative and intricate project only to realize you do not have the right tools to get the job done! The deep cut blade allows you to cut through thick cardstock, leather, chipboard and more. This blade is also compatible with the Explore Air 2 and the Maker machines. Do not forget; it is not only important to get the deep cut blade, but ensure you have the housing for it as well. It is recommended to purchase the blade before you think you will need it, so it is on hand any time you need it!

Save Money using Free SVG Files

It is a common misconception that you can only use Cricut design space files for your projects. You have many options when it comes to SVG designs for your projects. You can create your own in free software or even the Design Space center, or they can also be found all over the internet, for free! Many people create online content that is free for use for anyone that has a Cricut. It can not only save you money to utilize these free resources, but it can save you time as well since you are not creating the design yourself. Just make sure if you are using a design you find online that it is free to use for commercial use if you plan on selling or making money off of the project.

Other Pens work with the Explore Air Machine

This is another great way for you to save money on your projects. You are not only tied to using Cricut brand pens! You may need to invest in an accessory adapter, but you can save money using different brands of pens you can buy in bulk. These other brands

Design With Cricut

include but are not limited to Sharpie Pens and American Craft pens. Sharpies usually come in a variety pack including up to 24 different colors. You can now add perfect colored details to your projects without spending a fortune to get it.

Conclusion

Thank you for making it through to the end of *Design with Cricut*, let's hope it was informative and able to provide you with all of the tools you need to achieve your goals whatever they may be.

The next step is to use the information you have obtained for reading through the entirety of this book and applying it in practice with projects you are planning to do with your own Cricut machine. Feel free to refer to this book at any time if you feel like you need a refresher on what Cricut can do, what tool and accessories are available to you, as well as what machines can use what types of materials. Always remember that the Cricut Maker and the Explore Series give you a wide variety of options, but each machine does a different thing. We hope that with this book and knowledge you have gained from reading it, you are well on your way to becoming a professional at Cricut and truly enjoy using your creative mind to develop new projects.

This book was written with the sole purpose of helping new Cricut users become more familiar with the Cricut machine. We want to ensure everyone has an enjoyable experience when starting out with

Design With Cricut

Cricut. We hope we delivered on our objective as you finish this book. If you found this to be true, please feel free to recommend to friends, as this is how we get our book out to more people!

Finally, if you found this book useful in any way, a review on Amazon is always appreciated!

Design With Cricut

Connect with us on our Facebook page www.facebook.com/bluesourceandfriends and stay tuned to our latest book promotions and free giveaways.

Made in the USA
Coppell, TX
06 December 2019